Agenda
2019-
2020

ESTA AGENDA PERTENECE A:

_____

Enero

M	T	W	T	F	S	S
	1	2	3	4	5	6
7	8	9	10	11	12	13
14	15	16	17	18	19	20
21	22	23	24	25	26	27
28	29	30	31			

Febrero

M	T	W	T	F	S	S
				1	2	3
4	5	6	7	8	9	10
11	12	13	14	15	16	17
18	19	20	21	22	23	24
25	26	27	28			

Marzo

M	T	W	T	F	S	S
				1	2	3
4	5	6	7	8	9	10
11	12	13	14	15	16	17
18	19	20	21	22	23	24
25	26	27	28	29	30	31

Abril

M	T	W	T	F	S	S
1	2	3	4	5	6	7
8	9	10	11	12	13	14
15	16	17	18	19	20	21
22	23	24	25	26	27	28
29	30					

2019

Mayo

M	T	W	T	F	S	S
		1	2	3	4	5
6	7	8	9	10	11	12
13	14	15	16	17	18	19
20	21	22	23	24	25	26
27	28	29	30	31		

Junio

M	T	W	T	F	S	S
					1	2
3	4	5	6	7	8	9
10	11	12	13	14	15	16
17	18	19	20	21	22	23
24	25	26	27	28	29	30

Julio

M	T	W	T	F	S	S
1	2	3	4	5	6	7
8	9	10	11	12	13	14
15	16	17	18	19	20	21
22	23	24	25	26	27	28
29	30	31				

Agosto

M	T	W	T	F	S	S
			1	2	3	4
5	6	7	8	9	10	11
12	13	14	15	16	17	18
19	20	21	22	23	24	25
26	27	28	29	30	31	

Septiembre

M	T	W	T	F	S	S
						1
2	3	4	5	6	7	8
9	10	11	12	13	14	15
16	17	18	19	20	21	22
23	24	25	26	27	28	29
30						

Octubre

M	T	W	T	F	S	S
	1	2	3	4	5	6
7	8	9	10	11	12	13
14	15	16	17	18	19	20
21	22	23	24	25	26	27
28	29	30	31			

Noviembre

M	T	W	T	F	S	S
			1	2	3	
4	5	6	7	8	9	10
11	12	13	14	15	16	17
18	19	20	21	22	23	24
25	26	27	28	29	30	

Diciembre

M	T	W	T	F	S	S
						1
2	3	4	5	6	7	8
9	10	11	12	13	14	15
16	17	18	19	20	21	22
23	24	25	26	27	28	29
30	31					

2020

Enero

M	T	W	T	F	S	S
		1	2	3	4	5
6	7	8	9	10	11	12
13	14	15	16	17	18	19
20	21	22	23	24	25	26
27	28	29	30	31		

Febrero

M	T	W	T	F	S	S
					1	2
3	4	5	6	7	8	9
10	11	12	13	14	15	16
17	18	19	20	21	22	23
24	25	26	27	28	29	

Marzo

M	T	W	T	F	S	S
						1
2	3	4	5	6	7	8
9	10	11	12	13	14	15
16	17	18	19	20	21	22
23	24	25	26	27	28	29
30	31					

Abril

M	T	W	T	F	S	S
		1	2	3	4	5
6	7	8	9	10	11	12
13	14	15	16	17	18	19
20	21	22	23	24	25	26
27	28	29	30			

Mayo

M	T	W	T	F	S	S
				1	2	3
4	5	6	7	8	9	10
11	12	13	14	15	16	17
18	19	20	21	22	23	24
25	26	27	28	29	30	31

Junio

M	T	W	T	F	S	S
1	2	3	4	5	6	7
8	9	10	11	12	13	14
15	16	17	18	19	20	21
22	23	24	25	26	27	28
29	30					

Julio

M	T	W	T	F	S	S
		1	2	3	4	5
6	7	8	9	10	11	12
13	14	15	16	17	18	19
20	21	22	23	24	25	26
27	28	29	30	31		

Agosto

M	T	W	T	F	S	S
					1	2
3	4	5	6	7	8	9
10	11	12	13	14	15	16
17	18	19	20	21	22	23
24	25	26	27	28	29	30
31						

Septiembre

M	T	W	T	F	S	S
	1	2	3	4	5	6
7	8	9	10	11	12	13
14	15	16	17	18	19	20
21	22	23	24	25	26	27
28	29	30				

Octubre

M	T	W	T	F	S	S
			1	2	3	4
5	6	7	8	9	10	11
12	13	14	15	16	17	18
19	20	21	22	23	24	25
26	27	28	29	30	31	

Noviembre

M	T	W	T	F	S	S
						1
2	3	4	5	6	7	8
9	10	11	12	13	14	15
16	17	18	19	20	21	22
23	24	25	26	27	28	29
30						

Diciembre

M	T	W	T	F	S	S
	1	2	3	4	5	6
7	8	9	10	11	12	13
14	15	16	17	18	19	20
21	22	23	24	25	26	27
28	29	30	31			

AGOSTO

DOMINGO	LUNES	MARTES	MIERCOLES
4	5	6	7
11	12	13	14
18	19	20	21
25	26	27	28

2019

JUEVES	VIERNES	SABADO	NOTAS
1	2	3	
8	9	10	
15	16	17	
22	23	24	
29	30	31	

SEPTIEMBRE

DOMINGO	LUNES	MARTES	MIERCOLES
1	2	3	4
8	9	10	11
15	16	17	18
22	23	24	25
29	30		

2019

JUEVES	VIERNES	SABADO	NOTAS
5	6	7	
12	13	14	
19	20	21	
26	27	28	

OCTUBRE

DOMINGO	LUNES	MARTES	MIERCOLES
		1	2
6	7	8	9
13	14	15	16
20	21	22	23
27	28	29	30

2019

JUEVES	VIERNES	SABADO	NOTAS
3	4	5	
10	11	12	
17	18	19	
24	25	26	
31			

NOVIEMBRE

DOMINGO	LUNES	MARTES	MIERCOLES
3	4	5	6
10	11	12	13
17	18	19	20
24	25	26	27

2019

JUEVES	VIERNES	SABADO	NOTAS
	1	2	
7	8	9	
14	15	16	
21	22	23	
28	29	30	

DICIEMBRE

DOMINGO	LUNES	MARTES	MIERCOLES
1	2	3	4
8	9	10	11
15	16	17	18
22	23	24	25
29	30	31	

2 0 1 9

JUEVES	VIERNES	SABADO	NOTAS
5	6	7	
12	13	14	
19	20	21	
26	27	28	

ENERO

DOMINGO	LUNES	MARTES	MIERCOLES
			1
5	6	7	8
12	13	14	15
19	20	21	22
26	27	28	29

2020

JUEVES	VIERNES	SABADO	NOTAS
2	3	4	
9	10	11	
16	17	18	
23	24	25	
30	31		

FEBRERO

DOMINGO	LUNES	MARTES	MIERCOLES
2	3	4	5
9	10	11	12
16	17	18	19
23	24	25	26

2020

JUEVES	VIERNES	SABADO	NOTAS
		1	
6	7	8	
13	14	15	
20	21	22	
27	28	29	

MARZO

DOMINGO	LUNES	MARTES	MIERCOLES
1	2	3	4
8	9	10	11
15	16	17	18
22	23	24	25
29	30	31	

2020

JUEVES	VIERNES	SABADO	NOTAS
5	6	7	
12	13	14	
19	20	21	
26	27	28	

ABRIL

DOMINGO	LUNES	MARTES	MIERCOLES
			1
5	6	7	8
12	13	14	15
19	20	21	22
26	27	28	29

2020

JUEVES	VIERNES	SABADO	NOTAS
2	3	4	
9	10	11	
16	17	18	
23	24	25	
30			

MAYO

DOMINGO	LUNES	MARTES	MIERCOLES
3	4	5	6
10	11	12	13
17	18	19	20
24/31	25	26	27

2020

JUEVES	VIERNES	SABADO	NOTAS
	1	2	
7	8	9	
14	15	16	
21	22	23	
28	29	30	

JUNIO

DOMINGO	LUNES	MARTES	MIERCOLES
	1	2	3
7	8	9	10
14	15	16	17
21	22	23	24
28	29	30	

2020

JUEVES	VIERNES	SABADO	NOTAS
4	5	6	
11	12	13	
18	19	20	
25	26	27	

JULIO

DOMINGO	LUNES	MARTES	MIERCOLES
			1
5	6	7	8
12	13	14	15
19	20	21	22
26	27	28	29

2019

JUEVES	VIERNES	SABADO	NOTAS
2	3	4	
9.	10	11	
16	17	18	
23	24	25	
30	31		

Mi vision para el
2020

Mis metas para el
2020

1

2

3

4

5

6

7

8

9

10

CUMPLEAÑOS

ENERO	FEBRERO	MARZO

ABRIL	MAYO	JUNIO

JULIO	AGOSTO	SEPTIEMBRE

OCTUBRE	NOVIEMBRE	DICIEMBRE

PASSWORDS

WEB	USERNAME	PASSWORD

PASSWORDS

WEB	USERNAME	PASSWORD

CONTACTOS

NOMBRE	TELEFONO	EMAIL

CONTACTOS

NOMBRE	TELEFONO	EMAIL

Agosto

○ 29. LUNES

PRIORIDADES

○ 30. MARTES

○ 31. MIERCOLES

COSAS QUE HACER:

○ 1. JUEVES

○ 2. VIERNES

○ 3. SABADO/ 4. DOMINGO

Agosto

○ 5. LUNES

PRIORIDADES

○ 6. MARTES

○ 7. MIERCOLES

COSAS QUE HACER

○ 8. JUEVES

○ 9. VIERNES

○ 10. SABADO / 11.DOMINGO

Agosto

○ 12. LUNES

PRIORIDADES

○ 13. MARTES

○ 14. MIERCOLES

COSAS QUE HACER

○ 15. JUEVES

○ 16. VIERNES

○ 17. SABADO / 18. DOMINGO

Agosto

○ 19. LUNES

○ 20. MARTES

○ 21. MIERCOLES

COSAS QUE HACER

○ 22. JUEVES

○ 23. VIERNES

○ 24. SABADO /25.DOMINGO

Agosto Septiembre

○ 26. LUNES

PRIORIDADES

_____

_____

○ 27. MARTES

_____

_____

_____

○ 28. MIERCOLES

COSAS QUE HACER

_____

○ 29. JUEVES

_____

_____

_____

_____

○ 30. VIERNES

_____

_____

_____

○ 31. SABADO / 1. DOMINGO

_____

_____

_____

Septiembre

○ 2. LUNES

PRIORIDADES

○ 3. MARTES

○ 4. MIERCOLES

COSAS QUE HACER

○ 5. JUEVES

○ 6. VIERNES

○ 7. SABADO / 8.DOMINGO

Septiembre

○ 9. LUNES

PRIORIDADES

_____

_____

○ 10. MARTES

_____

_____

_____

_____

○ 11. MIERCOLES

COSAS QUE HACER

_____

_____

○ 12. JUEVES

_____

_____

_____

_____

○ 13.VIERNES

_____

_____

_____

_____

○ 14. SABADO /15. DOMINGO

_____

_____

_____

Septiembre

○ 16. LUNES

PRIORIDADES

○ 17. MARTES

○ 18.MIERCOLES

COSAS QUE HACER

○ 19. JUEVES

○ 20. VIERNES

○ 21. SABADO /22. DOMINGO

Septiembre

○ 23. LUNES

PRIORIDADES

○ 24. MARTES

○ 25. MIERCOLES

COSAS QUE HACER

○ 26. JUEVES

○ 27. VIERNES

○ 28. SABADO / 29. DOMINGO

Octubre

○ 30. LUNES

PRIORIDADES

○ 1. MARTES

○ 2. MIERCOLES

COSAS QUE HACER

○ 3. JUEVES

○ 4. VIERNES

○ 5. SABADO / 6. DOMINGO

Octubre

○ 7. LUNES

PRIORIDADES

_____

_____

○ 8. MARTES

_____

_____

_____

○ 9. MIERCOLES

COSAS QUE HACER

_____

○ 10. JUEVES

_____

_____

_____

_____

○ 11. VIERNES

_____

_____

_____

_____

○ 12. SABADO / 13. DOMINGO

_____

_____

_____

Octubre

○ 14. LUNES

○ 15. MARTES

○ 16. MIERCOLES

COSAS QUE HACER

○ 17. JUEVES

○ 18. VIERNES

○ 19. SABADO / 20. DOMINGO

Octubre

○ 21. LUNES

PRIORIDADES

○ 22. MARTES

○ 23. MIERCOLES

COSAS QUE HACER

○ 24. JUEVES

○ 25. VIERNES

○ 26. SABADO / 27. DOMINGO

Noviembre

○ 28. LUNES

PRIORIDADES

○ 29. MARTES

○ 30. MIERCOLES

COSAS QUE HACER

○ 31. JUEVES

○ 1. VIERNES

○ 2. SABADO / 3. DOMINGO

Noviembre

○ 4. LUNES

PRIORIDADES

_____

_____

○ 5. MARTES

_____

_____

_____

○ 6. MIERCOLES

COSAS QUE HACER

_____

○ 7. JUEVES

_____

_____

_____

_____

○ 8. VIERNES

_____

_____

_____

○ 9. SABADO /10. DOMINGO

_____

_____

_____

Noviembre

○ 11. LUNES

PRIORIDADES

_____

_____

○ 12. MARTES

_____

_____

_____

_____

○ 13. MIERCOLES

COSAS QUE HACER

_____

_____

○ 14. JUEVES

_____

_____

_____

_____

○ 15. VIERNES

_____

_____

_____

_____

○ 16.SABADO /17. DOMINGO

_____

_____

_____

Noviembre

○ 18. LUNES

PRIORIDADES

○ 19. MARTES

○ 20. MIERCOLES

COSAS QUE HACER

○ 21. JUEVES

○ 22. VIERNES

○ 23. SABADO / 24. DOMINGO

Noviembre Diciembre

○ 25. LUNES

PRIORIDADES

○ 26. MARTES

○ 27. MIERCOLES

COSAS QUE HACER

○ 28. JUEVES

○ 29. VIERNES

○ 30. SABADO / 1. DOMINGO

Diciembre

○ 2. LUNES

PRIORIDADES

_____

_____

○ 3. MARTES

_____

_____

_____

_____

○ 4. MIERCOLES

COSAS QUE HACER

_____

_____

○ 5. JUEVES

_____

_____

_____

_____

○ 6. VIERNES

_____

_____

_____

_____

○ 7. SABADO /8. DOMINGO

_____

_____

_____

Diciembre

○ 9. LUNES

PRIORIDADES

_____
_____
_____
_____
_____

○ 10. MARTES

○ 11. MIERCOLES

COSAS QUE HACER

_____
_____
_____
_____
_____

○ 12. JUEVES

_____
_____
_____

○ 13. VIERNES

_____
_____
_____
_____

○ 14. SABADO / 15. DOMINGO

_____
_____
_____
_____

Diciembre

○ 16. LUNES

PRIORIDADES

○ 17. MARTES

○ 18. MIERCOLES

COSAS QUE HACER

○ 19. JUEVES

○ 20. VIERNES

○ 21. SABADO / 22. DOMINGO

Diciembre

○ 23. LUNES

PRIORIDADES

○ 24. MARTES

○ 25. MIERCOLES

COSAS QUE HACER

○ 26. JUEVES

○ 27. VIERNES

○ 28. SABADO / 29. DOMINGO

Diciembre Enero

○ 30. LUNES

PRIORIDADES

○ 31. MARTES

○ 1. MIERCOLES

COSAS QUE HACER

○ 2. JUEVES

○ 3. VIERNES

○ 4. SABADO / 5. DOMINGO

Enero

○ 6. LUNES

PRIORIDADES

○ 7. MARTES

○ 8. MIERCOLES

COSAS QUE HACER

○ 9. JUEVES

○ 10. VIERNES

○ 11. SABADO / 12. DOMINGO

Enero

○ 13. LUNES

PRIORIDADES

○ 14. MARTES

○ 15. MIERCOLES

COSAS QUE HACER

○ 16. JUEVES

○ 17. VIERNES

○ 18. SABADO / 19. DOMINGO

Enero

○ 20. LUNES

PRIORIDADES

○ 21. MARTES

○ 22. MIERCOLES

COSAS QUE HACER

○ 23. JUEVES

○ 24. VIERNES

○ 25. SABADO / 26. DOMINGO

Enero Febrero

○ 27. LUNES

PRIORIDADES

_____

_____

○ 28. MARTES

_____

_____

_____

_____

○ 29. MIERCOLES

COSAS QUE HACER

_____

_____

○ 30. JUEVES

_____

_____

_____

_____

○ 31. VIERNES

_____

_____

_____

_____

○ 1.SABADO / 2. DOMINGO

_____

_____

_____

_____

Febrero

○ 3. LUNES

PRIORIDADES

○ 4. MARTES

○ 5. MIERCOLES

COSAS QUE HACER

○ 6. JUEVES

○ 7. VIERNES

○ 8. SABADO /9. DOMINGO

Febrero

○ 10. LUNES

PRIORIDADES

_____

_____

○ 11. MARTES

_____

_____

_____

_____

○ 12. MIERCOLES

COSAS QUE HACER

_____

_____

○ 13. JUEVES

_____

_____

_____

_____

○ 14. VIERNES

_____

_____

_____

_____

○ 15. SABADO /16. DOMINGO

_____

_____

_____

Febrero

○ 17. LUNES

PRIORIDADES

_____

_____

○ 18. MARTES

_____

_____

_____

_____

○ 19. MIERCOLES

COSAS QUE HACER

_____

_____

○ 20. JUEVES

_____

_____

_____

_____

_____

○ 21. VIERNES

_____

_____

_____

_____

_____

○ 22. SABADO / 23. DOMINGO

_____

_____

_____

Febrero Marzo

○ 24. LUNES

PRIORIDADES

_____

_____

○ 25. MARTES

_____

_____

_____

_____

○ 26. MIERCOLES

COSAS QUE HACER

_____

_____

○ 27. JUEVES

_____

_____

_____

_____

○ 28. VIERNES

_____

_____

_____

_____

○ 29. SABADO / 1. DOMINGO

_____

_____

_____

Marzo

○ 2. LUNES

○ 3. MARTES

○ 4. MIERCOLES

○ 5. JUEVES

○ 6. VIERNES

○ 7.SABADO / 8. DOMINGO

PRIORIDADES

_____
_____
_____
_____
_____
_____

COSAS QUE HACER

_____
_____
_____
_____
_____
_____
_____
_____
_____
_____
_____
_____

Marzo

○ 9. LUNES

PRIORIDADES

○ 10. MARTES

○ 11. MIERCOLES

COSAS QUE HACER

○ 12. JUEVES

○ 13. VIERNES

○ 14. SABADO / 15. DOMINGO

Marzo

○ 16. LUNES

○ 17. MARTES

○ 18. MIERCOLES

COSAS QUE HACER

○ 19. JUEVES

○ 20. VIERNES

○ 21.SABADO / 22. DOMINGO

Marzo

○ 23. LUNES

PRIORIDADES

○ 24. MARTES

○ 25. MIERCOLES

COSAS QUE HACER

○ 26. JUEVES

○ 27. VIERNES

○ 28. SABADO / 29. DOMINGO

Marzo Abril

○ 30. LUNES

PRIORIDADES

○ 31. MARTES

○ 1. MIERCOLES

COSAS QUE HACER

○ 2. JUEVES

○ 3. VIERNES

○ 4.SABADO / 5. DOMINGO

Abril

○ 6. LUNES

PRIORIDADES

_____

_____

○ 7. MARTES

_____

_____

_____

_____

○ 8. MIERCOLES

COSAS QUE HACER

_____

_____

○ 9. JUEVES

_____

_____

_____

_____

○ 10. VIERNES

_____

_____

_____

_____

○ 11. SABADO / 12. DOMINGO

_____

_____

_____

Abril

○ 13. LUNES

PRIORIDADES

○ 14. MARTES

○ 15. MIERCOLES

COSAS QUE HACER

○ 16. JUEVES

○ 17. VIERNES

○ 18. SABADO / 19. DOMINGO

Abril

○ 20. LUNES

                            PRIORIDADES

○ 21. MARTES

○ 22. MIERCOLES

                          COSAS QUE HACER

○ 23. JUEVES

○ 24. VIERNES

○ 25. SABADO / 26. DOMINGO

Abril Mayo

○ 27. LUNES

PRIORIDADES

○ 28. MARTES

○ 29. MIERCOLES

COSAS QUE HACER

○ 30. JUEVES

○ 1. VIERNES

○ 2. SABADO / 3. DOMINGO

Mayo

○ 4. LUNES

PRIORIDADES

_____

_____

○ 5. MARTES

_____

_____

_____

_____

○ 6. MIERCOLES

COSAS QUE HACER

_____

○ 7. JUEVES

_____

_____

_____

_____

○ 8. VIERNES

_____

_____

_____

_____

○ 9.SABADO / 10. DOMINGO

_____

_____

_____

Mayo

○ 11. LUNES

○ 12. MARTES

○ 13. MIERCOLES

○ 14. JUEVES

○ 15. VIERNES

○ 16. SABADO / 17. DOMINGO

PRIORIDADES

_____
_____
_____
_____
_____
_____

COSAS QUE HACER

_____
_____
_____
_____
_____
_____
_____
_____
_____
_____
_____
_____

Mayo

○ 18. LUNES

PRIORIDADES

○ 19. MARTES

○ 20. MIERCOLES

COSAS QUE HACER

○ 21. JUEVES

○ 22. VIERNES

○ 23. SABADO /24. DOMINGO

Mayo

○ 25. LUNES

PRIORIDADES

○ 26. MARTES

○ 27. MIERCOLES

COSAS QUE HACER

○ 28. JUEVES

○ 29. VIERNES

○ 30. SABADO / 31. DOMINGO

Junio

○ 1. LUNES

PRIORIDADES

_____

_____

○ 2. MARTES

_____

_____

_____

_____

○ 3. MIERCOLES

COSAS QUE HACER

_____

_____

○ 4. JUEVES

_____

_____

_____

_____

○ 5. VIERNES

_____

_____

_____

_____

○ 6. SABADO / 7. DOMINGO

_____

_____

_____

_____

Junio

○ 8. LUNES

PRIORIDADES

_____

_____

○ 9. MARTES

_____

_____

_____

_____

○ 10. MIERCOLES

COSAS QUE HACER

_____

○ 11. JUEVES

_____

_____

_____

_____

○ 12. VIERNES

_____

_____

_____

_____

○ 13. SABADO / 14. DOMINGO

_____

_____

_____

Junio

○ 15. LUNES

PRIORIDADES

○ 16. MARTES

○ 17. MIERCOLES

COSAS QUE HACER

○ 18. JUEVES

○ 19. VIERNES

○ 20. SABADO / 21. DOMINGO

Junio

○ 22. LUNES

PRIORIDADES

○ 23. MARTES

○ 24. MIERCOLES

COSAS QUE HACER

○ 25. JUEVES

○ 26. VIERNES

○ 27. SABADO / 28. DOMINGO

Junio Julio

○ 29. LUNES

PRIORIDADES

_____

_____

○ 30. MARTES

_____

_____

_____

_____

○ 1. MIERCOLES

COSAS QUE HACER

_____

○ 2. JUEVES

_____

_____

_____

_____

○ 3. VIERNES

_____

_____

_____

_____

○ 4. SABADO / 5. DOMINGO

_____

_____

_____

Julio

○ 6. LUNES

○ 7. MARTES

○ 8. MIERCOLES

COSAS QUE HACER

○ 9. JUEVES

○ 10. VIERNES

○ 11. SABADO / 12. DOMINGO

Julio

○ 13. LUNES

PRIORIDADES

○ 14. MARTES

○ 15. MIERCOLES

COSAS QUE HACER

○ 16. JUEVES

○ 17. VIERNES

○ 18. SABADO / 19. DOMINGO

Julio

○ 20. LUNES

PRIORIDADES

○ 21. MARTES

○ 22. MIERCOLES

COSAS QUE HACER

○ 23. JUEVES

○ 24. VIERNES

○ 25. SABADO / 26. DOMINGO

Julio

○ 27. LUNES

_____

○ 28. MARTES

_____

_____

_____

_____

○ 29. MIERCOLES

_____

COSAS QUE HACER

_____

○ 30. JUEVES

_____

_____

_____

_____

○ 31. VIERNES

_____

_____

_____

_____

○ 1.SABADO / 2. DOMINGO

_____

_____

_____

NOTAS